A Treasury of Songs

A Treasury of Songs

Songs by Julia Donaldson

Illustrated by Axel Scheffler

MACMILLAN CHILDREN'S BOOKS

Contents

Introduction
by Julia Donaldson

This book contains the words of twenty three of my children's songs, and you can hear the tunes on the CD that comes with it.

I wrote songs long before I started writing books and I still enjoy performing them when I visit schools, theatres and book festivals. You can hear some of these on the Gruffalo website, but I hope there will be plenty of new ones for you to discover here.

Several of the songs in this collection were written for children's television, including "A Squash and a Squeeze", which was later made into a book – my very first book, illustrated by the wonderful Axel Scheffler.

Axel and I have now been working together on picture books for over twenty years, and I hope that we will carry on for many more to come. I'm delighted with all the extra pictures that Axel has done to make this such a decorative book.

Once I started writing stories it felt natural to make up songs to go with them. You can find many of these "story songs" here, including "The Gruffalo", "Room on the Broom" and "The Snail and the Whale". One of the songs, "The World Inside a Book" was written to go with *Charlie Cook's Favourite Book*, but I like to think that the words can be changed to fit any book. Maybe you can choose a story you like and make up a new verse about it.

As well as the songs that go with my own books there are some others based on well-known Aesop's fables like "The Hare and the Tortoise" and "The Fox and the Crow". There are also plenty of action songs for you to join in with, such as "I've Got a Ball of Pastry". I wrote that one when my second son was at nursery school. I used to sing it with the children in his class, who liked pretending to roll pastry, peel bananas and toss pancakes.

I wrote the tunes of all the songs, but the musical arrangements that you can hear on the CD were written by Andrew Dodge, with whom I often worked in my television-writing days. Andrew also produced the CD and it was a great experience doing the recording with him, as I was accompanied by some wonderful professional musicians.

Once you've got to know the songs you can sing along on your own; or if you go to school maybe your class could sing some of them. I hope you'll enjoy joining in with the actions too.

If you play an instrument, you might be interested to know that the songs (plus a few others) also appear with a simple piano accompaniment and guitar chords in the three previously published collections, *The Gruffalo Song and Other Songs*, *Room on the Broom and Other Songs* and *The Gruffalo's Child and Other Songs*.

My thanks go to Axel Scheffler as well as to Andrew Dodge and all the musicians, and I'm really grateful to my niece Imogen and her daughters Lola and Amelie who sing on "The World Inside a Book" and "Stick Man". My husband Malcolm also sings on some of the songs, as well as joining the other musicians with his guitar, and to him go my extra special thanks, as I probably wouldn't have written nearly so many songs or stories without his encouragement and enthusiasm.

Happy reading, listening – and singing!

Julia Donaldson

A Squash and a Squeeze

A little old lady lived all by herself
With a table and chair and a jug on the shelf.
A wise old man heard her grumble and grouse,
"There's not enough room in my house."

She said, "Wise old man,
won't you help me, please?
My house is a squash and a squeeze."

"Take in your hen," said the wise old man.
"Take in my hen? What a curious plan."
Well, the hen laid an egg on the fireside rug,
And flapped round the room, knocking over the jug.
The little old lady cried, "What shall I do?
It was poky for one and it's tiny for two.
My nose has a tickle and there's no room to sneeze.
My house is a squash and a squeeze."

And she said, "Wise old man,
won't you help me, please?
My house is a squash and a squeeze."

"Take in your goat," said the wise old man.
"Take in my goat? What a curious plan."
Well, the goat chewed the curtains and trod on the egg,
Then sat down to nibble the table leg.
The little old lady cried, "Glory be!
It was tiny for two and it's titchy for three.
The hen pecks the goat and the goat's got fleas.
My house is a squash and a squeeze."

And she said, "Wise old man,
won't you help me, please?
My house is a squash and a squeeze."

"Take in your pig," said the wise old man.
"Take in my pig? What a curious plan."
So she took in the pig, who kept chasing the hen
And raiding the larder again and again.
The little old lady cried, "Stop, I implore!
It was titchy for three and it's teeny for four.
Even the pig in the larder agrees
My house is a squash and a squeeze."

And she said, "Wise old man,
won't you help me, please?
My house is a squash and a squeeze."

"Take in your cow," said the wise old man.
"Take in my cow? What a curious plan."
Well, the cow took one look and charged straight at the pig,
Then jumped on the table and tapped out a jig.
The little old lady cried, "Heavens alive!
It was teeny for four and it's weeny for five.
I'm tearing my hair out, I'm down on my knees,
My house is a squash and a squeeze."

And she said, "Wise old man,
won't you help me, please?
My house is a squash and a squeeze."

"Take them all out," said the wise old man.
"But then I'll be back where I first began."
So she opened the window and out flew the hen.
"That's better – at last I can sneeze again."
She shooed out the goat and she shoved out the pig.
"My house is beginning to feel pretty big."
She huffed and she puffed and she pushed out the cow.
"Just look at my house – it's enormous now.
Thank you, old man, for the work you have done.
It was weeny for five; it's gigantic for one.
There's no need to grumble and there's no need to grouse.
There's plenty of room in my house."

And now she's full of frolics
and fiddle-de-dees.
It isn't a squash
and it isn't a squeeze.
Yes, she's full of frolics
and fiddle-de-dees.
It isn't a squash or a squeeze.

Use Your Arms

Use your arms like a policeman:
make the traffic stop and go.

Use your arms like an archer:
shoot an arrow from your bow.

Use your arms like a strongman,
lifting up a heavy weight.

Use your arms like a scarecrow:
stick them out all stiff and straight.

Stretch, shrug,
Fold, hug:
Use your arms.
Use your arms.

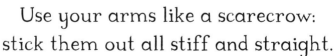

Use your arms like a mother:
rock your baby son or daughter.

Use your arms like a diver,
poised to plunge into the water.

Use your arms like a swimmer:
do the breast stroke, do the crawl.

Use your arms like a bowler,
running up to throw the ball.

Stretch, shrug,
Fold, hug:
Use your arms.
Use your arms.

Use your arms like a cowboy:
spin and twirl the old lasso.

Use your arms like a sailor,
hauling in a rope or two.

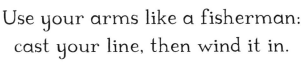

Use your arms like a fisherman:
cast your line, then wind it in.

Use your arms like a fiddler,
playing on your violin.

Stretch, shrug,
Fold, hug:
Use your arms.
Use your arms.
Use your arms.

Breathing Song

When you see a flower, do you sniff?
When you see a flower, do you sniff?
If it is a rose,
a lovely smell goes up your nose,
When you sniff,
When you sniff.

When you climb a hill, do you pant?
When you climb a hill, do you pant?
When you're at the top,
I bet you're really glad to stop,
And you pant,
And you pant.

When you get a shock, do you gasp?
When you get a shock, do you gasp?
Somebody says "Boo!"
or there's a spider on your shoe,
So you gasp,
So you gasp.

When you have a cold, do you sneeze?
When you have a cold, do you sneeze?
Nothing you can do can stop it;
here it comes – a-choo!
Yes, you sneeze,
Yes, you sneeze.

When your birthday comes, do you puff?
When your birthday comes, do you puff?
Maybe you can blow
the candles out in just one go,
When you puff,
When you puff.

When you're feeling sad, do you sigh?
When you're feeling sad, do you sigh?
No one wants to play,
and it's a cold and rainy day,
So you sigh,
So you sigh.

When you're feeling tired, do you yawn?
When you're feeling tired, do you yawn?
You grumbled when they said
that it was nearly time for bed,
But you yawn,
Yes, you yawn.

When you're fast asleep, do you snore?
When you're fast asleep, do you snore?
Have you got a snore
so loud it wakes them up next door,
When you snore,
When you snore?

The Gruffalo

He has terrible tusks and terrible claws
and terrible teeth in his terrible jaws.
He's the Gruffalo, Gruffalo, Gruffalo.
He's the Gruffalo.

He has knobbly knees and turned-out toes
and a poisonous wart at the end of his nose.
He's the Gruffalo, Gruffalo, Gruffalo.
He's the Gruffalo.

His eyes are orange. His tongue is black.
He has purple prickles all over his back.
He's the Gruffalo, Gruffalo, Gruffalo.
He's the Gruffalo, Gruffalo, Gruffalo.

He's the Grr...rr...rr...rr...ruffalo.

HE'S THE GRUFFALO!

Steering a Great Big Trolley

Steering a great big trolley
All round a great big shop.
Whoosh! Round the corners.
Whoops! Mind the customers.
Hold tight, we're going to stop.

Reach up high for the honey.
Reach down low for the ham.
Jar, tin and packet, watch how you stack it.
Don't break the strawberry jam!

Here we go again . . .

Steering a great big trolley
All round a great big shop.
Whoosh! Round the corners.
Whoops! Mind the customers.
Hold tight, we're going to stop.

Reach up high for the jelly.
Reach down low for the juice.
Jar, tin and packet, watch how you stack it.
Don't squash the chocolate mousse!

Here we go again . . .

Steering a great big trolley
All round a great big shop.
Whoosh! Round the corners.
Whoops! Mind the customers.
Cash desk – we're going to stop.

Out come jars, tins and packets.
Out comes money to pay.
Pack up the shopping, no time for stopping.
Goodbye, we're off on our way.
Goodbye, we're off on our way.

The Crow and the Fox

Fox on the ground, Crow in the trees.
Fox feeling hungry, Crow has some cheese.
Fox licks his lips, "Good morning, hello.
How do you do, you beautiful crow?"

Hush, silly bird, don't open your beak.
You'll lose that cheese if you speak.

Fox tries again, "Beautiful day,
Don't you agree? What do you say?
Elegant bird with feathers so sleek,
Can you be dumb? Why don't you speak?"

Hush, silly bird, don't open your beak.
You'll lose that cheese if you speak.

"Your wings and your tail are glossy and dark.
Your eyes are like diamonds, your voice like a lark.
Sing for me now! Oh, how I long
To hear just one note – won't you sing me a song?"

Hush, silly bird, don't open your beak.
You'll lose that cheese if you speak.

Crow feeling good, puffing with pride,
Eyes shining brightly, head on one side,
Opens her beak, lets out a sound – CAAAGH!
Down falls the cheese to Fox on the ground.

Hush, silly bird, why did you croak?
You lost that cheese when you spoke.

Fox on the ground, Crow in the trees,
Crow feeling hungry, Fox has the cheese.

Under the Water

Fish blow bubbles under the water.
Here's how the fish blow bubbles under the water.
Why don't you swim underwater with me?
Look through your goggles and see
How the fish blow bubbles under the water,
Down below.

Tadpoles wriggle under the water.
Here's how the tadpoles wriggle under the water.
Why don't you swim underwater with me?
Look through your goggles and see
How the tadpoles wriggle
And the fish blow bubbles under the water,
Down below.

Seaweed flutters under the water.
Here's how the seaweed flutters under the water.
Why don't you swim underwater with me?
Look through your goggles and see
How the seaweed flutters
And the tadpoles wriggle
And the fish blow bubbles under the water,
Down below.

Sharks eat fishes under the water.
Here's how the sharks eat fishes under the water.
Why don't you swim underwater with me?
Look through your goggles and see
How the sharks eat fishes
And the seaweed flutters
And the tadpoles wriggle
And the fish blow bubbles
Under the water, down below.

The Snail and the Whale

This is the tale,
The incredible tale of a snail and a whale.
This is the tale,
The incredible tale of a snail
Who sailed all round the world on the tail of a whale.

Land, sea and sky.
It was all so enormous it made the snail sigh.
Land, sea and sky.
"Oh, how terribly tiny am I,
Oh, how tiny am I," said the snail with a sigh.

Then came the day
When the whale lost his way and was beached in a bay.
Then came the day
When the water was slipping away
And he heavily, helplessly lay in the bay.

Here comes the snail.
Keep your eyes on the blackboard – she's leaving a trail.
Here comes the snail
And she writes on the board, "Save the whale."
"Save the whale," writes the snail with her silvery trail.

Dig, squirt and spray.
All the children and firemen are working away.
Dig, squirt and spray,
Till the tide rolls back into the bay
And the snail and the whale travel safely away.

Snail after snail
After snail slithers on to the tail of the whale.
Snail after snail
And they sing to the sea as they sail,
Yes, they sing as they sail on the tail of the whale.

I've Got a Ball of Pastry

I've got a ball of pastry.
What shall I do with that?

You've got to roll it, roll it, roll it,
Until you've rolled that pastry flat.
You've got to roll it, roll it, roll it,
Until you've rolled that pastry flat.

I've got a ripe banana.
Tell me where I begin.

You've got to peel it, peel it, peel it,
Until you've peeled off all the skin.
You've got to peel it, peel it, peel it,
Until you've peeled off all the skin.

I've got a pot of porridge,
Creamy and thick and hot.

You've got to stir it, stir it, stir it,
Until it's bubbling in the pot.
You've got to stir it, stir it, stir it,
Until it's bubbling in the pot.

I've got a jar of strawberry jam,
Sticky and sweet and red.

You've got to spread it, spread it, spread it,
Until it's on a slice of bread.
You've got to spread it, spread it, spread it,
Until it's on a slice of bread.

I've got a flat, round pancake.
One side has just been fried.

You've got to toss it, toss it, toss it,
Until it lands the other side.
You've got to toss it, toss it, toss it,
Until it lands the other side.

I've got a plate of dinner.
What do you think that's for?

You've got to eat it, eat it, eat it,
And if it's nice you'll ask for more.
You've got to eat it, eat it, eat it,
And if it's nice you'll ask for more. MORE!

The Smartest Giant
in Town

My tie is a scarf for a cold giraffe,
But look me up and down –
I'm the smartest giant in town.

My tie is a scarf for a cold giraffe,
My shirt's on a boat as a sail for a goat,
But look me up and down –
I'm the smartest giant in town.

My tie is a scarf for a cold giraffe,
My shirt's on a boat as a sail for a goat,
My shoe is a house for a little white mouse,
But look me up and down –
I'm the smartest giant in town.

My tie is a scarf for a cold giraffe,
My shirt's on a boat as a sail for a goat,
My shoe is a house for a little white mouse,
One of my socks is a bed for a fox,
But look me up and down –
I'm the smartest giant in town.

My tie is a scarf for a cold giraffe,
My shirt's on a boat as a sail for a goat,
My shoe is a house for a little white mouse,
One of my socks is a bed for a fox,
My belt helped a dog who was crossing a bog,
But . . . my trousers are falling down!
I'm the coldest giant in town!

Your tie is a scarf for a cold giraffe,
Your shirt's on a boat as a sail for a goat,
Your shoe is a house for a little white mouse,
One of your socks is a bed for a fox,
Your belt helped a dog who was crossing a bog,
So here is a very fine crown
To go with the sandals and gown
Of the KINDEST giant in town.

The Stick Man Song

Stick Man lives in the family tree
With his Stick Lady Love and their stick children three.
One day he wakes early and goes for a jog.
Stick Man, oh Stick Man, beware of the dog!

Come back home, we're missing you, Stick Man!
Come back home to the family tree.
Come back home, we're missing you, Stick Man!
Come back home to the family tree.

"A stick!" cries a girl with a smile on her face.
"The right kind of Pooh-stick for winning the race!"
"A twig!" says a swan. "This twig is the best!
It's the right kind of twig to weave into my nest."

Come back home, we're missing you, Stick Man!
Come back home to the family tree.
Come back home, we're missing you, Stick Man!
Come back home to the family tree.

"A mast!" cries a dad. "An excellent mast!
Hooray! There's a flag on our castle at last."
"I'm not a mast for a silly old flag.
Or a sword for a knight, or a hook for a bag."

"An arm!" says a boy with a warm woolly scarf.
"An arm for my snowman," he says with a laugh.
"A stick!" cries a mum. "A stick for the grate!"
Wake up, Stick Man, before it's too late!

Come back home, we're missing you, Stick Man!
Come back home to the family tree.
Come back home, we're missing you, Stick Man!
Come back home to the family tree.

But what is this chuckle that turns to a shout?
"Oh-ho-ho ho-ho . . . I'm STUCK! Get me OUT!"
A Stuck Man? *A Stuck Man?* Now who could that be?
"Don't worry!" says Stick Man, "I'll soon set you free."

Come back home, we're missing you, Stick Man!
Come back home to the family tree.
Come back home, we're missing you, Stick Man!
Come back home to the family tree.

Then Stick Man helps Santa deliver the toys
To fast-asleep girls and to fast-asleep boys.
Faster and faster they fly through the snow,
Till Santa says, "Only one chimney to go!"

Stick Lady's lonely. The children are sad.
It won't feel like Christmas without their Stick Dad.
But who is this tumbling into their house?
Is it a bird, or a bat, or a mouse?

Or could it be, or could it be Stick Man,
Come back home to the family tree?
Yes it is! It really is Stick Man,
Sticking here in the family tree!

The Mouse and the Lion

In the hottest sun of the longest day,
A lion lay down for a doze.
A little brown mouse pattered out to play,
Pit-a-pat, pit-a-pat, he danced on
the whiskery nose.
Pit-a-pat, pit-a-pat, pit-a-pat, pit-a-pat,
He danced on the whiskery nose.

The lion awoke with a sneeze, "A-choo!"
He picked up the mouse in his paw.
"And who may I venture to ask are you?
Grrrrrr!" he said with a terrible roar.
"Grr, grrr, grrrrr, GRRRRRR!"
He said with a terrible roar.

"I'll save your life if you'll let me go,"
The mouse's voice shook as he spoke.
The lion laughed loudly, "Oho, oho, ohohohoho!
I'll let you go free for your joke.
Oho, oho, ohohohoho,
I'll let you go free for your joke."

As chance would have it, the following week,
The lion was caught in a net.
When all of a sudden he heard a squeak:
"Squeak, squeak, well met, noble lion, well met.
Squeak, squeak, squeak, squeak,
Well met, noble lion, well met."

The little mouse nibbled and gnawed and bit
Till the lion was finally free.
"It's nothing, dear lion, don't mention it:
Nibbly, nibble, I'm repaying your kindness to me.
Nibbly, nibbly, nibbly, nibble,
Repaying your kindness to me."

For one of the lessons which mice must learn
From their whiskery father and mother
Is the famous old saying that one good turn
Always deserves another.
Pit-a-pat! Grrr! Ohoho! Squeak!
Always deserves another.

The Hare
and the Tortoise

The hare was the handsomest hare in the world,
With a white fluffy bobtail and whiskers that curled.
He lived in a field, and his favourite sport was
Leapfrogging over the back of the tortoise.
The hare went a-loping, a-lolloping, a-leaping.
The tortoise went crawling, a-creaking, a-creeping.

The hare claimed that no one was faster than he.
He asked all the animals, "Who'll race with me?"
The tortoise said, "I will!" The hare roared with laughter.
"Race with a tortoise? Why, what could be dafter?
I'll go a-loping, a-lolloping, a-leaping.
You'll come a-crawling, a-creaking, a-creeping."

They mapped out a course and they fixed on a day.
It's one-two-three go! and the hare is away,
Whisking his bobtail and frisking and gambolling.
Way back behind him the tortoise is ambling.
The hare goes a-loping, a-lolloping, a-leaping.
The tortoise comes crawling, a-creaking, a-creeping.

The hare is half-way when he stretches and blinks.
"I've nothing to lose if I snatch forty winks."
His head drops, his eyes close, and soon he is slumbering.
Inching towards him the tortoise is lumbering.
The hare is a-snoring, a-snoozing, a-sleeping.
The tortoise comes crawling, a-creaking, a-creeping.

The hare wakes and starts: is it real or a ghost?
The tortoise is nearing the finishing post.

The hare helterskelters but just doesn't do it.
Slowcoach the tortoise has beaten him to it.

The hare lost a-snoring, a-snoozing, a-sleeping.
The tortoise won crawling, a-creaking, a-creeping.

Room on the Broom

I am a cat, as LEAN as can be.
Is there room on the broom for a cat like me?
Yes, yes, yes!

I am a dog, as KEEN as can be.
Is there room on the broom for a dog like me?
Yes, yes, yes!

I am a bird, as GREEN as can be.
Is there room on the broom for a bird like me?
Yes, yes, yes!

I am a frog, as CLEAN as can be.
Is there room on the broom for a frog like me?
Yes, yes . . .
No!

I am a dragon, as MEAN as can be.
Is there room on the broom for a dragon like me?
NO, NO, NO!
OFF YOU GO!
Ho ho ho ho ho ho HO!

Keep on the Go

Jump about. Keep on the go.
Jump about and don't go slow.
Let's see who can jump about the most,
And we'll soon be warm as toast.

Jump about and pat your head. Keep on the go.
Jump about and pat your head and don't go slow.
Let's see who can jump about and
pat their head the most,
And we'll soon be warm as toast.

Jump about and pat your head
and shake yourself. Keep on the go.
Jump about and pat your head
and shake yourself and don't go slow.
Let's see who can jump about and
pat their head and shake themselves the most,
And we'll soon be warm as toast.

Jump about and pat your head and shake yourself
and roll your eyes. Keep on the go.
Jump about and pat your head and shake yourself
and roll your eyes and don't go slow.
Let's see who can jump about
and pat their head and shake themselves
and roll their eyes the most,
And we'll soon be warm as toast.

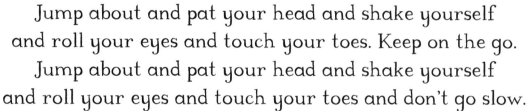

Jump about and pat your head and shake yourself
and roll your eyes and touch your toes. Keep on the go.
Jump about and pat your head and shake yourself
and roll your eyes and touch your toes and don't go slow.
Let's see who can jump about and
pat their head and shake themselves and roll their eyes
and touch their toes the most,
And we'll soon be warm as toast.

Monkey Puzzle

My mum isn't a great grey hunk.
She's got no tusks and she's got no trunk.
She doesn't hiss and she doesn't croak.
Butterfly, butterfly, please don't joke.

It's a monkey puzzle.
Butterfly, butterfly, can't you see?
It's a monkey puzzle.
None of these animals looks like me.

My mum doesn't have lots of legs.
She's got no beak and she can't lay eggs.
She doesn't flitter about all night.
Butterfly, butterfly, get it right.

It's a monkey puzzle.
Butterfly, butterfly, can't you see?
It's a monkey puzzle.
None of these animals looks like me.

Here comes someone with fingers and toes
And very long arms and a nice pink nose,
A curly tail and a furry tum.
Butterfly, butterfly - that's NOT Mum!

It's a monkey puzzle.
Butterfly, butterfly, are you mad?
It's a monkey puzzle.
That's not my mummy - no, that's my dad!

What's Your Colour?

What's your colour, the colour of your skin,
The colour of the envelope that you're wrapped in?

Is it like chocolate, tea or coffee?
Is it like marzipan, fudge or toffee?
Peaches and cream or a strawberry milkshake?
Or covered in moles like a curranty cake?

What's your colour, the colour of your skin,
The colour of the envelope that you're wrapped in?

Are you a map of your past disasters?
Grazes and scratches and sticking plasters?
Bites from mosquitoes, a yellow-blue bruise?
And a couple of blisters from rather tight shoes?

What's your colour, the colour of your skin,
The colour of the envelope that you're wrapped in?

How does it go when the weather's sunny?
Brown as a berry or gold as honey?
Does it go freckly or peeling and sore?
Is there a mark from the watch that you wore?

What's your colour, the colour of your skin,
The colour of the envelope that you're wrapped in?

Do you go pink when you're all embarrassed?
Sweaty and red when you're hot and harassed?
Bumpy and blue on a cold winter's day?
When it's time for your bath are you usually grey?

What's your colour, the colour of your skin,
The colour of the envelope that you're wrapped in?

Nut Tree

Small, brown, hard, round,
The nut is lying underground.

Now a shoot begins to show.
Now the shoot begins to grow.

Tall, taller, tall as can be,
The shoot is growing into a tree.

And branches grow and stretch and spread,
With twigs and leaves above your head.

And on a windy autumn day,
The nut tree bends, the branches sway.

The leaves fly off and whirl around,
And nuts go tumbling to the ground.
Small, brown, hard, round . . .

The Gruffalo's Child

Where are you going to, Gruffalo's Child,
All by yourself through the woods so wild?
Aha! Oho!
To look for the Big Bad Mouse.

Where can he be? I'll ask the Snake.
He's down by the lake, eating Gruffalo cake.
Aha! Oho!
Beware of the Big Bad Mouse.

Where can he be? Will Owl tell me?
He's under a tree, drinking Gruffalo tea.
Too-whit! Too-whoo!
Beware of the Big Bad Mouse.

Where can he be? The Fox looks sly:
He's somewhere nearby, eating Gruffalo pie.
Aha! Oho!
Beware of the Big Bad Mouse.

Who is this creature so big and strong?
His tail and his whiskers are terribly long.
Oh help! Oh no!
It must be the Big Bad Mouse!

Where are you going to, Gruffalo's Child,
All by yourself through the woods so wild?
Away! Back home!
To hide from the Big Bad Mouse.

Funny Face

Pull a funny face.
Move your eyes and nose and mouth
all over the place.

First you smile like a clown,
Then you turn the corners down,
Bare your teeth, open wide,
Move your jaws from side to side.

Pull a funny face.
Move your eyes and nose and mouth
all over the place.

Raise your eyebrows, roll your eyes,
Make them grow to twice their size,
Shut them tight, wink and blink,
Keep them open just a chink.

Pull a funny face.
Move your eyes and nose and mouth
all over the place.

Make your face long and thin,
Give yourself a double chin,
Twitch your nose, frown and pout,
Suck your cheeks in, puff them out.

Pull a funny face.
Move your eyes and nose and mouth
all over the place.

The Wind and the Sun

Said the wind to the sun, "I can carry off kites
And howl down the chimney on blustery nights.
I can sail boats and set windmills in motion,
Rattle the windows and ruffle the ocean."

And the old sun grinned
At the wild winter wind.

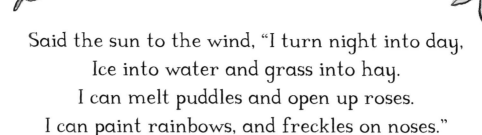

Said the sun to the wind, "I turn night into day,
Ice into water and grass into hay.
I can melt puddles and open up roses.
I can paint rainbows, and freckles on noses."

And the old sun grinned
At the wild winter wind.

Said the wind to the sun, "You'll be sorry you spoke.
Down on the road is a man with a cloak.
If you're so clever then let's see you prove it.
We'll take it in turns to see who can remove it."

And the old sun grinned
At the wild winter wind.

The wind blew the trees till the boughs bent and broke.
He bowled the man's hat off and howled round his cloak.
He blew and he blustered, he tossed and he tugged it.
The man wrapped it round him and tightly he hugged it.

And the old sun grinned
At the wild winter wind.

"Take a rest," said the sun. "Let me shine on him now."
He shone till the man started mopping his brow.
The man settled down in the shade of some boulders.
He undid his cloak and it slipped from his shoulders.

And the old sun grinned
At the wild winter wind.

Shuffle and Squelch

Spring brings showers; the world's aflood.
Wellies on, let's brave the mud.
We'll go squelching about, squelching about,
Squelching about in the mud.

Yes, we'll go squelching about,
squelching about,
Squelching about in the mud.

Kick your boots off, everyone.
Summer's here and so's the sun.
We'll go dancing about, dancing about,
Dancing about in the sun.

Yes, we'll go dancing about,
dancing about,
Dancing about in the sun.

Hold your hat, the winds are thieves.
Watch them steal the autumn leaves.
As we shuffle about, shuffle about,
Shuffle about in the leaves.

Yes, we can shuffle about,
shuffle about,
Shuffle about in the leaves.

Wind your scarf round once or twice,
Winter's turned the pond to ice.
We'll go sliding about, sliding about,
Sliding about on the ice.

Yes, we'll go sliding about,
sliding about,
Sliding about on the ice.

The World Inside a Book

There is a world inside a book.
And when you're curled up with a book,
It doesn't matter what your age is,
You can take a flying leap into the pages.
So take a leap, and take a look
Inside the world inside a book.

There is a world inside my book.
And when I'm curled up with my book,
I meet a pirate, a wicked pirate,
And I dig up lots of treasure with the pirate.
You can dig too, just take a look
Inside the world inside my book.

There is a world inside my book.
And when I'm curled up with my book,
I meet a dragon, a fiery dragon,
And I help a shining knight to fight the dragon.
You can help too, just take a look
Inside the world inside my book.

There is a world inside my book.
And when I'm curled up with my book,
I meet a spaceman, a famous spaceman,
And I fly off in a rocket with the spaceman.
You can fly too, just take a look
Inside the world inside my book.

There is a world inside my book.
And when I'm curled up with my book,
I meet a lady, a headless lady,
And I glide about a castle with the lady.
You can glide too, just take a look
Inside the world inside my book.

There is a world inside a book.
And when you're curled up with a book,
It doesn't matter what your age is,
You can take a flying leap into the pages.
So take a leap, and take a look
Inside the world inside a book.

First published 2016 by Macmillan Children's Books
an imprint of Pan Macmillan
20 New Wharf Road, London N1 9RR
Associated companies throughout the world
www.panmacmillan.com
ISBN: 978-1-4472-8271-6